**THIS JOURNAL
BELONGS TO:**

RISEN MOTHERHOOD
GUIDED JOURNAL

EMILY JENSEN & LAURA WIFLER

HARVEST HOUSE PUBLISHERS
EUGENE, OREGON

Published in association with the literary agency of Wolgemuth & Associates.

Cover design by Nicole Dougherty
Interior design by Janelle Coury
Illustrations by Emilie Mann

For bulk, special sales, or ministry purchases, please call 1-800-547-8979.
Email: Customerservice@hhpbooks.com

RISEN MOTHERHOOD GUIDED JOURNAL

Copyright © 2023 by Emily Jensen and Laura Wifler
Published by Harvest House Publishers
Eugene, Oregon 97408
www.harvesthousepublishers.com

ISBN 978-0-7369-8789-9 (pbk.)

Printed in Colombia

23 24 25 26 27 28 29 30 31 / NI / 10 9 8 7 6 5 4 3 2 1

CONTENTS

Part 3: How Do I Learn to Apply the Gospel in Motherhood?

A NOTE FROM EMILY AND LAURA

Dear friend,

As moms, we have a lot of things to prepare and organize. We pack school bags and lunchboxes. We stuff little pockets with snacks and hand over full water bottles—reminding busy kiddos to go potty because there is not going to be another chance for a long time! With all the things we manage and remember for others, it can be tough to keep our own things straight. And that's exactly why we created this *Risen Motherhood Guided Journal*.

We've been to book clubs and Bible studies ourselves, and we know what it feels like to lose track of all those stray papers. We know that sometimes, not having a space to write is a barrier to completing your discussion questions (even if in theory, it shouldn't be). We know that a little hand or a budding writer might swipe your pen and doodle all over your notes if you leave them lying around. So, Mama, this journal is just for you.

Having the discussion questions beautifully laid out with plenty of space to write and process might be just the tool you need to spend more time thinking about the gospel in your life. This practical hack isn't just good for checking the box; it's an important part of thinking deeply about God's Word and how it comes to bear on your life today. Even though you're used to the rush, we pray that this journal will be a reminder to sit and linger over the things that really matter for eternity.

You'll never regret investing time in your relationship with the Lord, asking him to help you understand his truth and live it out. We hope this journal can be a helpful part of that process, making gospel thinking just a tiny bit easier.

Joyfully,
Emily & Laura

HOW TO USE
THIS GUIDED JOURNAL

This guided journal is designed as a tool to help you work through the *Risen Mother-hood* book. We pray this journal makes it easier for you to process what you're learning as you read and provides a chance for you to put your gospel-thinking muscles into practice by applying the gospel story to your own unique circumstances. Here's how to use it.

1. **Read the chapter.** As you read, don't get caught up in the examples or personal experiences of Emily or Laura if you don't relate. Take what's helpful and focus on the underlying principles.

2. **Answer the discussion questions.** In this section, you'll find the book's discussion questions as well as two additional questions for each chapter that are not found in the book. As you respond, write down any additional questions or thoughts you want to explore on your own or discuss with friends or family.

3. **Try the Personal Practice.** This area is designed for you to write down your personal situation related to the chapter topic and think about how the gospel applies. After you write down your own circumstance, you'll find space for you to funnel it through the four parts of the gospel: creation, fall, redemption, consummation. For guidance, Emily and Laura write about how they do this in chapter 2 of the *Risen Motherhood* book.

4. **Fill out the Gospel Truths section.** If you've listened to the *Risen Motherhood* podcast, you know that Emily and Laura love using hymns, poems, and quotes to inspire and encourage their walk with the Lord. This space is designed for you to write down any meaningful songs or writings that you come across related to the chapter topic.

5. **Write down a prayer.** This section can be used to write down personal prayer requests related to the chapter, or you can write down the prayers of your book club or moms' group if you're working through this journal with a group.

6. **Go at your own pace.** This journal isn't meant to be a burden. Go at your own (or your book club's!) cadence, and allow the Spirit to work in your heart and mind as you consider the truths found in the book.

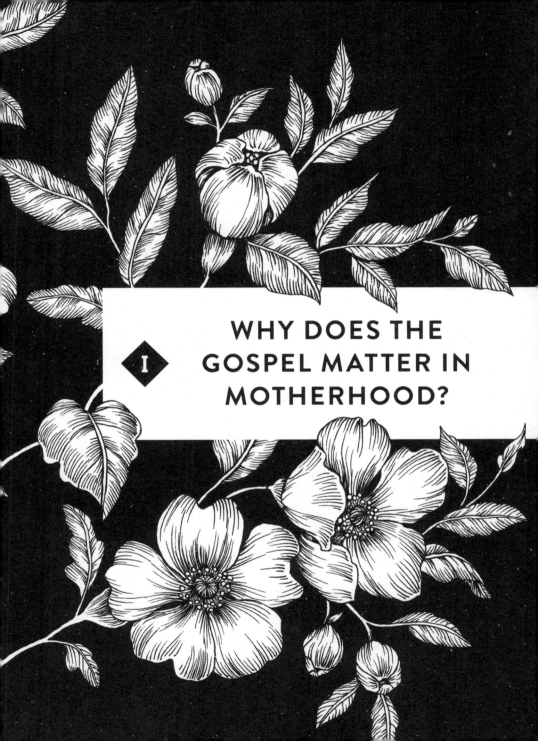

WHY DOES THE GOSPEL MATTER IN MOTHERHOOD?

I

WHAT IS THE GOSPEL?

Emily and Laura

Discussion Questions

1. How has your background contributed to your feelings about or understanding of the gospel?

_____

_____

_____

_____

_____

_____

_____

2. Write down the gospel story in your own words.

_____

_____

_____

_____

_____

_____

_____

3. Have you believed the good news and put your faith in Christ's death and resurrection? If so, what hope do you have today and forever?

_____

_____

_____

_____

_____

_____

_____

_____

4. Where have you been doing battle in motherhood? Considering what you've learned about the gospel, describe the actual battleground and the real enemy.

_____

_____

_____

_____

_____

_____

_____

_____

_____

5. What area of the gospel would you like to learn more about? Why?

_____

_____

_____

_____

_____

_____

_____

_____

_____

_____

God blessed them. And God said to them,
"Be fruitful and multiply and fill the
earth and subdue it, and have dominion
over the fish of the sea and over the
birds of the heavens and over every living
thing that moves on the earth."

GENESIS 1:28

PERSONAL PRACTICE

My Situation

_____

_____

_____

_____

_____

_____

Creation

_____

_____

_____

_____

_____

Fall

_____

_____

_____

_____

_____

Redemption

_____

_____

_____

_____

_____

_____

_____

_____

Consummation

_____

_____

_____

_____

_____

_____

_____

_____

17

Gospel Truths

_____

_____

_____

_____

_____

_____

_____

_____

PRAYERS

_____

_____

_____

_____

_____

_____

_____

_____

_____

_____

GOD'S PURPOSE
FOR MOTHERHOOD

Emily and Laura

Discussion Questions

1. We all come into motherhood with unique paradigms and conclusions for our role as a mom. How, or by whom, have yours been shaped? What are some of the primary things you believe define a mom's purpose?

2. Can you summarize God's purpose for motherhood in your own words? How does that compare with your idea of the ideal mom?

3. In what ways have you personally seen the effects of the fall in your motherhood? Where does God want you to turn during hard things, when you feel discouraged about your inability to measure up?

_____

_____

_____

_____

_____

_____

_____

4. In what ways does knowing that "Christ has perfectly fulfilled everything expected of us as mothers" give you hope?

_____

_____

_____

_____

_____

_____

_____

5. Where do you need God's help to live out his purpose today?

_____

_____

_____

_____

_____

_____

_____

_____

_____

_____

_____

The Spirit of the Lord is upon me,
   because he has anointed me
   to proclaim good news to the poor.
He has sent me to proclaim liberty to the captives
   and recovering of sight to the blind,
   to set at liberty those who are oppressed.

LUKE 4:18

PERSONAL PRACTICE

My Situation

_____

_____

_____

_____

_____

_____

Creation

_____

_____

_____

_____

_____

Fall

_____

_____

_____

_____

_____

Redemption

_____

_____

_____

_____

_____

_____

_____

_____

Consummation

_____

_____

_____

_____

_____

_____

_____

_____

_____

Gospel Truths

_____

_____

_____

_____

_____

_____

_____

_____

PRAYERS

_____

_____

_____

_____

_____

_____

_____

_____

_____

_____

GOSPEL HOPE FOR THE EVERYDAY MOMENTS OF MOTHERHOOD

II

THE GOSPEL AND OUR HEART ATTITUDES

Laura

Discussion Questions

1. How do you react when things don't go your way? How does your response reflect what you worship?

_____

_____

_____

_____

_____

2. In what ways do you try to control life by managing your outside environment? How can you submit your desire for control to God? Where can you redirect your hope?

_____

_____

_____

_____

_____

_____

3. What is one area where you can choose to place your joy in Christ and not in your ever-changing environment? What specific steps can you take today to change?

_____

_____

_____

_____

_____

_____

_____

4. Name one spiritual discipline you'd like to work on to practice putting your trust in Christ.

_____

_____

_____

_____

_____

_____

_____

5. What name do you define yourself by? ("I am the angry mom," "I'm the worrier," "I'm the stressed-out mom"...) How does knowing that you are united with Christ, Christ *in* you, change the narrative of how you think about yourself?

_____

_____

_____

_____

_____

_____

_____

_____

I in them and you in me, that they may become perfectly one, so that the world may know that you sent me and loved them even as you loved me.

JOHN 17:23

PERSONAL PRACTICE

My Situation

_____

_____

_____

_____

_____

_____

Creation

_____

_____

_____

_____

_____

Fall

_____

_____

_____

_____

_____

Redemption

_____

_____

_____

_____

_____

_____

_____

_____

Consummation

_____

_____

_____

_____

_____

_____

_____

_____

Gospel Truths

_____

_____

_____

_____

_____

_____

_____

PRAYERS

_____

_____

_____

_____

_____

_____

_____

_____

_____

THE GOSPEL
AND OUR TRANSITIONS

Emily

Discussion Questions

1. What transition are you in right now, and how are you coping with the stress it brings?

_____

_____

_____

_____

_____

2. In what ways are you experiencing "pain, discomfort, awkwardness, false starts, and conflict" in your current transition? What are the specific pinch points?

_____

_____

_____

_____

_____

_____

3. How might God be working in your transition, making it about more than just survival? What areas of sin and idolatry do you see that you weren't aware of before, and what will you do about them?

_____

_____

_____

_____

_____

_____

_____

4. What is one of the better things you're looking forward to in the midst of this transition, and how might that longing be fully realized in heaven?

_____

_____

_____

_____

_____

_____

_____

_____

_____

5. Knowing this isn't a throwaway season, what will you thank God for today?

_____

_____

_____

_____

_____

_____

_____

_____

_____

In this you rejoice, though now for a little while, if necessary, you have been grieved by various trials, so that the tested genuineness of your faith—more precious than gold that perishes though it is tested by fire—may be found to result in praise and glory and honor at the revelation of Jesus Christ.

PERSONAL PRACTICE

My Situation

_____

_____

_____

_____

_____

_____

Creation

_____

_____

_____

_____

_____

Fall

_____

_____

_____

_____

_____

Redemption

_____

_____

_____

_____

_____

_____

_____

_____

Consummation

_____

_____

_____

_____

_____

_____

_____

_____

_____

Gospel Truths

_____

_____

_____

_____

_____

_____

_____

PRAYERS

_____

_____

_____

_____

_____

_____

_____

_____

_____

THE GOSPEL
AND OUR MARRIAGES

Laura

Discussion Questions

1. Do you impose any standards on your husband for what an involved Christian dad looks like? How do your standards compare with God's?

_____

_____

_____

_____

_____

_____

2. Christ loved us so much, he gave up his life for ours. In what ways should Christ's sacrificial love motivate your own love toward your husband?

_____

_____

_____

_____

_____

_____

3. Regardless of where your husband is at with the Lord, what are areas of God's grace in his life? What is he doing "right" in parenting?

_____

_____

_____

_____

_____

_____

_____

_____

4. What are some things you can prayerfully work on in the way you view and interact with your husband?

_____

_____

_____

_____

_____

_____

_____

5. In what ways are you and/or your husband overcomplicating discipleship with your children? Or if your tendency is to take a more relaxed approach, what are some ways you can be sure you are weaving the gospel into everyday life?

_____

_____

_____

_____

_____

_____

_____

_____

_____

_____

If anyone would come after me, let him deny himself and take up his cross and follow me.

MARK 8:34

PERSONAL PRACTICE

My Situation

_____

_____

_____

_____

_____

_____

Creation

_____

_____

_____

_____

_____

Fall

_____

_____

_____

_____

_____

Redemption

_____

_____

_____

_____

_____

_____

_____

_____

_____

Consummation

_____

_____

_____

_____

_____

_____

_____

_____

_____

Gospel Truths

_____

_____

_____

_____

_____

_____

_____

_____

PRAYERS

_____

_____

_____

_____

_____

_____

_____

_____

_____

THE GOSPEL AND OUR MUNDANE MOMENTS

Emily

Discussion Questions

1. What's one of your least favorite mundane activities in motherhood? How would you describe how it makes you feel, and why does it make you feel that way?

_____

_____

_____

_____

_____

2. What is something you feel you "deserve" because of the mundane work or moments you've endured in motherhood? Where did you first get the idea that you deserved that, or can you trace back the roots of that idea? Is it from Scripture, or culture?

_____

_____

_____

_____

_____

3. How does Jesus identify with you in that mundane activity, and how does your role in God's redemptive story give that activity new purpose?

_____

_____

_____

_____

_____

_____

_____

4. Picture one of your mundane moments or activities and imagine how God might use that to bring about his good plans and purposes for others. How does the potential of your investment give you hope and faith in what God is doing?

_____

_____

_____

_____

_____

_____

_____

5. How will you show God's character to those around you today or this week as you complete your mundane activity?

_____

_____

_____

_____

_____

_____

_____

_____

_____

From him and through him
and to him are all things.
To him be glory forever.
Amen.

ROMANS 11:36

PERSONAL PRACTICE

My Situation

_____

_____

_____

_____

_____

_____

Creation

_____

_____

_____

_____

_____

Fall

_____

_____

_____

_____

_____

Redemption

_____

_____

_____

_____

_____

_____

_____

_____

Consummation

_____

_____

_____

_____

_____

_____

_____

_____

_____

Gospel Truths

_____

_____

_____

_____

_____

_____

_____

_____

PRAYERS

_____

_____

_____

_____

_____

_____

_____

_____

_____

_____

THE GOSPEL AND OUR BIRTH EXPERIENCES

Laura

Discussion Questions

1. As you reflect on or prepare for an upcoming birth, what are your expectations? Are any of them too idealistic in light of the fall?

2. In what ways does the childbirth process reflect your greater inner needs and weaknesses? How does the gospel meet you with hope?

3. What mercies can you find in your labor and delivery, and how can this cause you to worship?

_____

_____

_____

_____

_____

_____

_____

_____

4. When thinking about your childbirth(s), do you fall into one of the ditches of pride or despair? How has or might God use childbearing for your sanctification?

_____

_____

_____

_____

_____

_____

_____

_____

5. What threads of the gospel story do you see in childbearing? Write down a few that stuck out to you from the chapter or additional ones that come to mind.

We know that the whole creation has been groaning together in the pains of childbirth until now. And not only the creation, but we ourselves, who have the firstfruits of the Spirit, groan inwardly as we wait eagerly for adoption as sons, the redemption of our bodies.

ROMANS 8:22-23

PERSONAL PRACTICE

My Situation

_____

_____

_____

_____

_____

_____

Creation

_____

_____

_____

_____

_____

_____

Fall

_____

_____

_____

_____

_____

_____

Redemption

_____

_____

_____

_____

_____

_____

_____

_____

Consummation

_____

_____

_____

_____

_____

_____

_____

_____

Gospel Truths

_____

_____

_____

_____

_____

_____

_____

_____

PRAYERS

_____

_____

_____

_____

_____

_____

_____

_____

_____

_____

_____

THE GOSPEL AND OUR POSTPARTUM BODY IMAGE

Emily

Discussion Questions

1. How have you struggled with postpartum body image? Is it a big part of your thought life or your actions? Why or why not?

_____

_____

_____

_____

_____

2. In what specific ways have you been tempted to or tried to erase the marks of life-giving or the marks of motherhood (both literal and metaphorical)?

_____

_____

_____

_____

_____

_____

_____

3. What does God want you to focus on and devote your time to? How do God's values change how you view your body?

_____

_____

_____

_____

_____

_____

_____

_____

4. Spend a few minutes writing down at least six things you can thank God for about your body. Keep going if you can!

_____

_____

_____

_____

_____

_____

_____

_____

_____

5. Taking your time, resources, and limitations into account, how will you steward your body as a gift from God?

_____

_____

_____

_____

_____

_____

_____

_____

_____

_____

We are his workmanship,
created in Christ Jesus
for good works, which
God prepared beforehand,
that we should walk
in them.

EPHESIANS 2:10

PERSONAL PRACTICE

My Situation

_____

_____

_____

_____

_____

_____

Creation

_____

_____

_____

_____

_____

Fall

_____

_____

_____

_____

_____

Redemption

_____

_____

_____

_____

_____

_____

_____

_____

Consummation

_____

_____

_____

_____

_____

_____

_____

_____

Gospel Truths

_____

_____

_____

_____

_____

_____

_____

_____

PRAYERS

_____

_____

_____

_____

_____

_____

_____

_____

_____

_____

THE GOSPEL AND
OUR FOOD CHOICES

Laura

Discussion Questions

1. In what ways do you view food as a measuring stick of your ability to be a good mother?

_____

_____

_____

_____

_____

2. How does your identity in Christ remove the need for food-related worry, leading you instead to worship God for his provision and goodness in your life? Is there a specific area of misplaced worship you need to repent of?

_____

_____

_____

_____

_____

_____

3. How does the freedom of the gospel empower you to extend grace to others with different food preferences, and who can you do that for today?

_____

_____

_____

_____

_____

_____

_____

_____

4. Read Romans 14. What does Paul say about food? How can you apply that to an area of food that you worry about?

_____

_____

_____

_____

_____

_____

_____

_____

_____

5. What is one way you can choose to receive the food God has provided your family with thanksgiving? Write down a note of gratitude to the Lord.

_____

_____

_____

_____

_____

_____

_____

_____

_____

_____

On this mountain the LORD of hosts will make for all peoples
a feast of rich food, a feast of well-aged wine,
of rich food full of marrow, of aged wine well refined.

ISAIAH 25:6

PERSONAL PRACTICE

My Situation

_____

_____

_____

_____

_____

_____

Creation

_____

_____

_____

_____

_____

Fall

_____

_____

_____

_____

_____

Redemption

_____

_____

_____

_____

_____

_____

_____

Consummation

_____

_____

_____

_____

_____

_____

_____

_____

_____

Gospel Truths

_____

_____

_____

_____

_____

_____

_____

_____

PRAYERS

_____

_____

_____

_____

_____

_____

_____

_____

_____

_____

THE GOSPEL AND OUR RELATIONSHIPS

Emily

Discussion Questions

1. What relationships (friends, grandparents, coworkers...) have been most challenging to you in motherhood and why? How much are the challenges due to your personal preferences as opposed to specific, ongoing sin?

_____

_____

_____

_____

_____

2. In the context of challenging relationships, where have you been tempted to buy into culture's idea of how to confront or deal with conflicts or differences?

_____

_____

_____

_____

_____

_____

3. In what ways have you failed to live up to God's standards? How has he dealt with this in Christ? How should that change the way you relate in your challenging relationships?

_____

_____

_____

_____

_____

_____

_____

_____

4. Spend a few minutes writing down some relational or personal differences that you're grateful for in the lives of other moms. How do their different personalities, perspectives, and practices encourage you in your motherhood?

_____

_____

_____

_____

_____

_____

_____

5. Consider an upcoming situation where you might experience relational strain. How could you proactively pray, plan, and speak truth so you're ready to handle it with grace, truth, and love?

_____

_____

_____

_____

_____

_____

_____

_____

_____

Good sense makes one slow to anger,
and it is his glory to overlook an offense.

PROVERBS 19:11

PERSONAL PRACTICE

My Situation

_____

_____

_____

_____

_____

_____

Creation

_____

_____

_____

_____

_____

Fall

_____

_____

_____

_____

_____

Redemption

_____

_____

_____

_____

_____

_____

_____

_____

Consummation

_____

_____

_____

_____

_____

_____

_____

_____

_____

Gospel Truths

_____

_____

_____

_____

_____

_____

_____

_____

_____

PRAYERS

_____

_____

_____

_____

_____

_____

_____

_____

_____

_____

THE GOSPEL AND OUR TRADITIONS

Laura

Discussion Questions

1. How much pressure do you feel when celebrating family traditions? Do those celebrations sometimes define your status as a good mom? If so, how?

_____

_____

_____

_____

_____

2. How does knowing your standing is secure in Christ change the way you view your family's traditions and how you feel when they don't go according to plan?

_____

_____

_____

_____

_____

_____

_____

_____

3. Do your family's traditions point to God as your greatest treasure and testimony? What adjustments might you make to display him more fully?

_____

_____

_____

_____

_____

_____

_____

_____

4. What fruit have you seen from family traditions? Take time to thank God for his work in your family's life.

_____

_____

_____

_____

_____

_____

_____

_____

_____

5. The chapter notes how a tradition is anything you do with regularity in order to pass down information. Biblically, we find that it has the added significance of remembering God. Are there any traditions that you and your family engage in that don't remember God? How can you adjust them to make God known?

_____

_____

_____

_____

_____

_____

_____

_____

You will not delight in sacrifice, or I would give it;
  you will not be pleased with a burnt offering.
The sacrifices of God are a broken spirit;
  a broken and contrite heart,
  O God, you will not despise.

PSALM 51:16-17

PERSONAL PRACTICE

My Situation

_____

_____

_____

_____

_____

_____

Creation

_____

_____

_____

_____

_____

Fall

_____

_____

_____

_____

_____

Redemption

_____

_____

_____

_____

_____

_____

_____

_____

Consummation

_____

_____

_____

_____

_____

_____

_____

_____

Gospel Truths

_____

_____

_____

_____

_____

_____

_____

_____

PRAYERS

_____

_____

_____

_____

_____

_____

_____

_____

_____

_____

THE GOSPEL AND OUR CHRISTIAN COMMUNITY

Emily

Discussion Questions

1. What is your hope for community in motherhood, and how does that picture line up with God's plan for community?

_____

_____

_____

_____

_____

2. Can you think of a time when the church supported you in motherhood or in a previous season of life? How did that support bless and encourage you, even if it wasn't exactly the type of support you were looking for?

_____

_____

_____

_____

_____

_____

3. Do your heart and actions reflect Christ's heart for his church? Even though it's flawed, what ultimately makes the church beautiful and fruitful?

_____

_____

_____

_____

_____

_____

_____

_____

_____

4. How can you find, commit to, or further invest in your local church community, even in this busy season of motherhood?

_____

_____

_____

_____

_____

_____

_____

_____

5. How could you serve and encourage other moms in your church by sharing some of the gospel principles you're learning through this book?

_____

_____

_____

_____

_____

_____

_____

_____

_____

_____

On this rock I will build my church,
and the gates of hell shall not prevail against it.

MATTHEW 16:18

PERSONAL PRACTICE

My Situation

_____

_____

_____

_____

_____

_____

Creation

_____

_____

_____

_____

_____

Fall

_____

_____

_____

_____

_____

Redemption

_____

_____

_____

_____

_____

_____

_____

_____

Consummation

_____

_____

_____

_____

_____

_____

_____

_____

_____

Gospel Truths

_____

_____

_____

_____

_____

_____

_____

PRAYERS

_____

_____

_____

_____

_____

_____

_____

_____

_____

THE GOSPEL
AND OUR SERVICE

Laura

Discussion Questions

1. Do you tend to lean toward serving your family or serving others? How do your natural tendencies align to God's call to service?

_____

_____

_____

_____

_____

2. You're not made righteous by your actions. How does knowing this free you from trying to earn favor or feeling burdened when serving?

_____

_____

_____

_____

_____

_____

_____

3. What are some specific ways you can model Christ's life of service to others today? What would it look like to use that service as a training ground for your children?

_____

_____

_____

_____

_____

_____

_____

_____

4. We know that Christ serves us right now through the Holy Spirit. How does that give you courage to engage in service right where you are?

_____

_____

_____

_____

_____

_____

_____

_____

5. Look up Luke 12:37. Christ told his followers that he will continue to serve his people at the second coming and for eternity. What does it mean to you to know that God will serve you in this way?

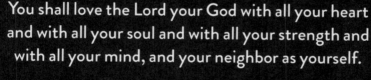

You shall love the Lord your God with all your heart and with all your soul and with all your strength and with all your mind, and your neighbor as yourself.

LUKE 10:27

PERSONAL PRACTICE

My Situation

_____

_____

_____

_____

_____

_____

Creation

_____

_____

_____

_____

_____

Fall

_____

_____

_____

_____

_____

Redemption

_____

_____

_____

_____

_____

_____

_____

_____

Consummation

_____

_____

_____

_____

_____

_____

_____

_____

_____

Gospel Truths

_____

_____

_____

_____

_____

_____

_____

PRAYERS

_____

_____

_____

_____

_____

_____

_____

_____

_____

THE GOSPEL AND OUR SELF-CARE

Emily

Discussion Questions

1. What's your ideal version of self-care? Do you have enough margin in your life to engage in it right now? If not, what barriers do you face?

_____

_____

_____

_____

_____

2. How do you react when your self-care strategies fall through? What does that reveal about your heart? If you rarely take enough time for rest or self-care, what might that reveal about your worship and beliefs?

_____

_____

_____

_____

_____

_____

3. Even if you don't have time for traditional methods of self-care, have you stopped to pray and trust God with your deepest needs? How is he sustaining you?

_____

_____

_____

_____

_____

_____

_____

_____

4. What is one way you'd like to better honor God's design for your need for rest? What is one area of self-care that you want to be more willing to let go of or lay down as you make time to serve others?

_____

_____

_____

_____

_____

_____

_____

_____

5. Write down three ways that Jesus Christ gives you rest now and three ways he will give you ultimate rest in the life to come.

_____

_____

_____

_____

_____

_____

_____

_____

_____

Rising very early in the morning, while it was still dark, he departed and went out to a desolate place, and there he prayed.

MARK 1:35

PERSONAL PRACTICE

My Situation

_____

_____

_____

_____

_____

_____

Creation

_____

_____

_____

_____

_____

Fall

_____

_____

_____

_____

_____

Redemption

_____

_____

_____

_____

_____

_____

_____

_____

Consummation

_____

_____

_____

_____

_____

_____

_____

_____

_____

Gospel Truths

_____

_____

_____

_____

_____

_____

_____

_____

PRAYERS

_____

_____

_____

_____

_____

_____

_____

_____

_____

_____

THE GOSPEL AND OUR CHILDREN WITH DIFFERENCES

Laura

Discussion Questions

1. If you are a mother of a child with differences, where do you tend to place your hope? If you are a friend of a mother in that situation, where do you encourage her to place her hope? How does this align with where the gospel tells us to place our hope?

_____

_____

_____

_____

_____

2. God promises to use our suffering for our sanctification and to draw us closer to him. How does this give you hope and encouragement when you receive a challenging diagnosis? In what ways is God making you new?

_____

_____

_____

_____

_____

3. How does the gospel bid you to display the works of God to those around you, using your unique situation to show the deep joy you have in Christ?

_____

_____

_____

_____

_____

_____

_____

4. Take a look at the verses Laura uses in the last section. What verse is particularly encouraging to you? Why?

_____

_____

_____

_____

_____

_____

_____

5. List some ways you've seen God's glory through your child with differences. How can you see God's work being displayed through their life and your situation?

_____

_____

_____

_____

_____

_____

_____

_____

He will wipe away every tear from their eyes, and death shall be no more, neither shall there be mourning, nor crying, nor pain anymore, for the former things have passed away.

REVELATION 21:4

PERSONAL PRACTICE

My Situation

_____

_____

_____

_____

_____

_____

Creation

_____

_____

_____

_____

_____

Fall

_____

_____

_____

_____

_____

Redemption

_____
_____
_____
_____
_____
_____
_____
_____

Consummation

_____
_____
_____
_____
_____
_____
_____
_____
_____

Gospel Truths

_____

_____

_____

_____

_____

_____

_____

_____

PRAYERS

_____

_____

_____

_____

_____

_____

_____

_____

_____

_____

THE GOSPEL AND OUR SCHOOLING CHOICES

Emily

Discussion Questions

1. Imagine the intersections in your child's life. What schooling paths do you see, and what do the destination signs read (if I choose X, then my child will Y)? What gave you those stereotypes, fears, and expectations?

_____

_____

_____

_____

_____

2. How might the discipleship of your children change as you keep the potential pitfalls or concerns of each schooling style in view? How could these concerns become teaching opportunities as you point your children to Christ?

_____

_____

_____

_____

_____

3. What secure hope can you have when you don't know your child's destination in life?

_____

_____

_____

_____

_____

_____

_____

_____

4. Regardless of school choice, how will you infuse the gospel into your child's everyday life, making Christ the culture and aroma of your home?

_____

_____

_____

_____

_____

_____

_____

_____

5. Regardless of school choice, what might it look like to love other parents, children, and teachers in your community, encouraging and praying for them on a regular basis?

_____

_____

_____

_____

_____

_____

_____

_____

_____

You shall teach [these laws] diligently to your children, and shall talk of them when you sit in your house, and when you walk by the way, and when you lie down, and when you rise. You shall bind them as a sign on your hand, and they shall be as frontlets between your eyes. You shall write them on the doorposts of your house and on your gates.

DEUTERONOMY 6:7-9

PERSONAL PRACTICE

My Situation

_____

_____

_____

_____

_____

_____

Creation

_____

_____

_____

_____

_____

Fall

_____

_____

_____

_____

_____

Redemption

_____

_____

_____

_____

_____

_____

_____

_____

_____

Consummation

_____

_____

_____

_____

_____

_____

_____

_____

_____

Gospel Truths

_____

_____

_____

_____

_____

_____

_____

_____

PRAYERS

_____

_____

_____

_____

_____

_____

_____

_____

_____

_____

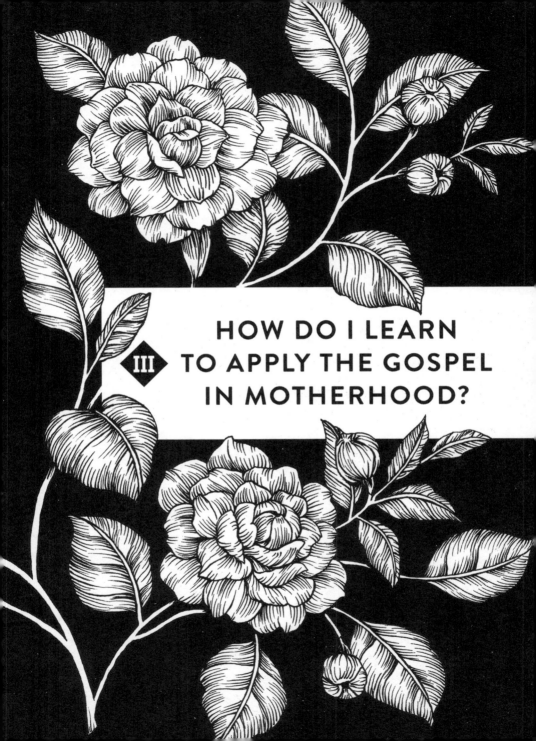

HOW DO I LEARN TO APPLY THE GOSPEL IN MOTHERHOOD?

III

ARE THE LITTLE YEARS
THE LOST YEARS?

Emily and Laura

Discussion Questions

1. What excuses do you make about faithfulness in the little years? How might your expectations of growth in God's Word need to change in this season?

2. How does the gospel offer you freedom from guilt yet motivate you to be stubborn—and to keep coming back to God's Word?

3. Are there areas of Bible literacy and gospel growth that you choose not to pursue because they're hard? What adjustments might you make to invest in Bible literacy in the amounts of time you have available?

_____

_____

_____

_____

_____

_____

_____

4. List some ways you *have* seen God grow you in Bible literacy over the years. Take time to thank him for his faithfulness!

_____

_____

_____

_____

_____

_____

_____

5. Where do you hope to be five years from now in your Bible literacy? What subject areas do you hope to grow in? What's one step you can take to do that in this season?

_____

_____

_____

_____

_____

_____

_____

_____

Abide in me, and I in you. As the branch cannot bear fruit by itself, unless it abides in the vine, neither can you, unless you abide in me. I am the vine; you are the branches. Whoever abides in me and I in him, he it is that bears much fruit, for apart from me you can do nothing

PERSONAL PRACTICE

My Situation

_____

_____

_____

_____

_____

_____

Creation

_____

_____

_____

_____

_____

Fall

_____

_____

_____

_____

_____

Redemption

_____

_____

_____

_____

_____

_____

_____

_____

Consummation

_____

_____

_____

_____

_____

_____

_____

_____

Gospel Truths

_____

_____

_____

_____

_____

_____

_____

_____

PRAYERS

_____

_____

_____

_____

_____

_____

_____

_____

_____

5. Consider a particular area of concern for you in your motherhood right now. Emily and Laura write, "God wants us to do what images him most clearly, worships him most fully, and loves other image-bearers most sacrificially." How can you apply the gospel to "make the best use of your time" in your current circumstance?

_____

_____

_____

_____

_____

_____

_____

_____

Look carefully then how you walk, not as unwise but as wise, making the best use of the time, because the days are evil.

EPHESIANS 5:15-16

PERSONAL PRACTICE

My Situation

_____

_____

_____

_____

_____

_____

Creation

_____

_____

_____

_____

_____

Fall

_____

_____

_____

_____

_____

Redemption

_____

_____

_____

_____

_____

_____

_____

_____

_____

Consummation

_____

_____

_____

_____

_____

_____

_____

_____

_____

Gospel Truths

_____

_____

_____

_____

_____

_____

_____

_____

PRAYERS

_____

_____

_____

_____

_____

_____

_____

_____

_____

_____

NOTES

NOTES

ABOUT THE AUTHORS

Emily Jensen and **Laura Wifler** are the cofounders of the Risen Motherhood ministry and cohosts of the chart-topping podcast. They are also in the trenches of motherhood, right alongside their readers. With a combination of accessibility, relatability, and solid biblical knowledge, Emily and Laura have a knack for simplifying complex scriptural truths, relating and applying them to everyday life. God has consistently and powerfully used the voices of these two moms to captivate women around the world with the gospel. As sisters-in-law, Emily and Laura both live in central Iowa with their families.

Connect with us:
🅞 emilyajensen
🅞 laurawifler

THE RISEN MOTHERHOOD
COMMUNITY

In a world full of opinions, how-tos, and silver-bullet solutions, Risen Motherhood offers a countercultural message to relieve the world's burdens placed on moms through the good news of the gospel. At Risen Motherhood, we believe moms can faithfully live out their calling in freedom as they know God's will through his Word. To this end, Risen Motherhood creates podcasts, articles, and free Bible study resources to equip, encourage, and challenge mothers to live in the light of the gospel.

Join the Risen Motherhood Community:

RisenMotherhood.com

 risenmotherhood

Risen Motherhood

RisenMotherhood.com/book